MW01713929

ITALIAN *Cuisine*

Berryland Books

0 9 8 7 6 5 4 3

Managing Editor: Richard Johnston
Author: Dr. Anita Shan
Designer: Prof. Madhu Krishna, Signet Designs, India.

Printed and bound in China
ISBN 1-84577-648-810

A catalogue record of this book is available from the British Library

NB: Recipes using uncooked eggs or meat or fish should be avoided by infants, the elderly, pregnant women and anyone suffering from an illness.

Contents

Deep-fried rice balls

Makes 10

Ingredients

- 5oz (150g) Mozzarella (or Gorgonzola)
- 1½oz (50g) parmesan
- 9½oz (300g) short-grain rice
- 2 eggs
- 16fl oz (½ litre) water
- 2tbsp (30ml) butter
- 4tbsp (60ml) breadcrumbs
- 2tbsp (30ml) flour
- 1 small packet saffron
- Salt & freshly ground pepper as desired
- Clarified butter or oil for deep-frying
- Bay leaves to garnish

Method

1 Bring to the boil 16fl oz (½ litre) salted water, sprinkle the rice into the boiling water and cook over a very low heat, stirring frequently, until the water has been absorbed. Dissolve the saffron in 2tbsp (30ml) hot water and stir into the rice along with the parmesan. Leave to cool slightly then stir in 2tbsp (30ml) butter and 1 egg.

2 Beat 1 egg in a deep plate and season lightly with salt and pepper.

3 Finely dice the cheese. Form the cooled rice into 10 balls about the size of a mandarin orange. Make a depression in the centre with your finger and fill with about 1tbsp (15ml) of cheese. Seal the opening with rice. Dust the rice balls with flour and dip first in egg and then in breadcrumbs. Lay carefully on a cloth.

4 Heat the clarified butter or oil in a deep pan and fry the rice balls, a few at a time. Drain on absorbent kitchen paper, then arrange on a serving plate with bay leaves. Serve with rocket and tomato salad.

Mussel gratin

Serves 4

Ingredients

- 48oz (1½ kg) fresh mussels
- 1 bunch flat-leaf parsley
- 5 cloves garlic
- 3 plum tomatoes
- 9tbsp (135ml) olive oil
- 6fl oz (200ml) dry white wine
- Freshly ground pepper as desired
- 1tsp (5ml) salt
- A pinch of cayenne pepper
- 2½oz (80g) breadcrumbs
- 2½oz (80g) grated pecorino or parmesan
- Coarse salt

Method

1 Scrub the mussels thoroughly under running water and remove the beards. Discard any mussels that are open.

2 Rinse the parsley, dry and finely chop the leaves. Peel the garlic cloves. Halve 2 cloves and chop the others. Wash and halve the tomatoes (from top to bottom), remove the seeds with a teaspoon and dice the flesh.

3 Heat 3tbsp (45ml) olive oil in a large pan and briefly sauté the halved garlic and parsley. Add the diced tomatoes and the mussels and deglaze with the white wine. Season with ½tsp (5ml) salt, pepper and cayenne pepper.

4 Cover with a lid and steam the mussels over a high heat until they open, shaking the pan from time to time so that the mussels cook evenly. Do not use any mussels that remain closed.

5 Drain the opened mussels. Separate the two halves of the mussels and place the halves containing the cooked mussel meat on a baking tray.

6 Preheat the grill. Sauté the chopped garlic in the rest of the oil, being careful not to let it burn. Add the parsley, breadcrumbs, pecorino (or parmesan) and salt and mix well.

7 Put a little of the cheese mixture on top of each mussel and press lightly. Put the tray of mussels under the grill for 5 minutes.

8 To serve, arrange the mussels on a serving platter thickly sprinkled with coarse salt. Serve warm or cold.

Pork escalopes with gratin topping

Serves 4

Ingredients

- 4 pork escalopes [not too thin, each weighing about 5oz (150g)]
- 1tbsp (15ml) oil
- 4tbsp (60ml) basil pesto (ready-made)
- 4 small courgettes
- ½ bunch basil
- 4 small tomatoes
- 1½oz (50g) cream
- Salt & freshly ground pepper as desired
- 5oz (150g) (1 ball) mozzarella
- Oil for the dish
- Tomato wedges to garnish

Method

1 Season the escalopes with salt and pepper. Heat the oil in a frying pan and fry the escalopes for about 1 minute each side. Take out of the pan, lay in an oiled baking dish and spread with pesto.

2 Wash, trim and coarsely grate the courgettes. Wash the tomatoes and cut into quarters or eighths. Mix the tomatoes with the cream, grated courgettes and basil. Season with salt and pepper and spread over the escalopes. Thinly slice the mozzarella and place on top of the escalopes.

3 Bake in a preheated oven [400°F (200°C), middle shelf] for about 15 - 20 minutes. Serve garnished with tomato wedges.

Mixed salad with tuna

Serves 4

Ingredients

- 9½oz (300g) frozen beans
- 3 tins tuna
- 2 red onions
- 16oz (500g) tomatoes
- 1 head romaine lettuce
- 20 black olives
- 2tsp (10ml) mustard
- 4tbsp (60ml) white wine vinegar
- Salt & pepper as desired
- 2tsp (10ml) capers
- 10tbsp (150ml) olive oil
- 1 bunch parsley

Method

1 Cook the frozen beans according to the instructions on the packet and drain. Drain the tuna and break up into largish pieces. Wash and quarter the tomatoes. Peel the onions and cut into thin rings. Wash the lettuce and divide into individual leaves. Arrange all the prepared ingredients and the olives on a large platter.

2 For the dressing, mix the mustard with the vinegar. Chop the capers very finely and stir in. Gradually beat in the oil. Season to taste with salt and pepper.

3 Wash the parsley, dry, chop finely and stir into the dressing. Sprinkle the dressing over the salad shortly before serving.

Italian pasta salad with tomatoes, mozzarella, basil

Serves 4

Ingredients

- 9½oz (300g) cherry tomatoes
- 1 mozzarella ball 4-5oz (125–150g)
- ½ bunch basil
- 1 shallot
- 3tbsp (45ml) red wine vinegar
- Salt & freshly ground pepper as desired
- A pinch of sugar
- 1 clove garlic
- 5tbsp (75ml) olive oil
- 9½oz (300g) penne

Method

1 Wash and quarter the tomatoes. Dice the mozzarella. Strip the basil leaves from the stalks. Peel and finely dice the shallot.

2 Mix the vinegar with the salt, pepper and sugar. Peel the garlic and press into the vinegar. Beat the olive oil into the dressing with a whisk. Mix the prepared ingredients with the dressing and leave to stand for about 30 minutes.

3 Cook the pasta in plenty of boiling, salted water until 'al dente', then drain, refresh in cold water and drain thoroughly. Carefully stir the tomato and mozzarella mixture into the pasta.

Aceto
Olio

Mozzarella salad

Serves 4

Ingredients

- Mixed salad leaves of your choice
- 8oz (250g) cocktail tomatoes
- 8oz (250g) mozzarelline (small mozzarella balls)
- Salt as desired
- Freshly ground pepper as desired
- 4tbsp (60ml) olive oil
- Lemon juice (from 1 large lemon)

Method

1 Wash the salad leaves and dry. Wash and halve the tomatoes. Drain the mozzarella balls.

2 Mix the salad leaves with the tomatoes, 4tbsp (60ml) olive oil, salt, pepper and lemon juice. Arrange on plates and top with mozzarella. Season with pepper and serve immediately.

Artichoke salad

Serves 4

Ingredients

- 4 small tender artichokes
- 1 lemon
- Salt as desired
- 1 fennel bulb
- ½ bunch parsley
- A couple of rocket leaves
- 1 clove garlic
- 1tbsp (15ml) capers
- 4tbsp (60ml) olive oil
- Freshly ground pepper as desired

Method

1 Carefully remove the outer leaves from the artichokes. Cut the sharp points off the rest of the leaves and peel the stalks to a point. Slice the artichokes very thinly lengthways, using a mandolin if available. Squeeze ½ lemon and mix the juice in with the artichoke slices. Salt lightly and leave to stand for about 15 minutes.

2 Wash and clean the fennel and reserve the tender leaves. Halve the bulb, remove the stalk and slice thinly lengthways. Add the fennel to the artichokes.

3 Wash the parsley and the rocket, dry, pick off the leaves and chop finely. Peel and finely chop the garlic. Peel the other half of the lemon, removing the white pith, and dice the flesh. Remove the seeds.

4 Chop the herbs with the fennel leaves, garlic, lemon flesh, capers and olive oil in a vegetable chopper. Season the dressing with salt and pepper and mix with the vegetables. If necessary, add more lemon juice.

Provencal tomato soup

Serves 2

Ingredients

- 12½oz (400g) fresh tomatoes or canned chopped tomatoes
- ½ onion
- 1 clove garlic
- 2tbsp (30ml) olive oil
- 1tsp (5ml) oregano
- 3fl oz (100ml) vegetable stock
- 1tsp (5ml) tomato puree
- 1 bay leaf
- Salt as desired
- Freshly ground pepper as desired
- 2 sprigs of basil
- ½tsp (2½ml) balsamic vinegar

Method

1 Scald, peel and halve the tomatoes and dice the flesh.

2 Peel and finely chop the onion and the garlic. Heat 1tbsp (15ml) olive oil in a pan and sauté the onion and garlic until translucent. Add the oregano. Stir in the tomatoes and the tomato puree. Add the vegetable stock, the bay leaf, salt and pepper. Bring the soup to a boil, cover with a lid and simmer for about 5 minutes.

3 Wash the basil and dry. Put 4 leaves aside for garnishing. Cut the rest of the leaves into fine strips.

4 Puree the soup with a hand blender. Mix in the chopped basil, then season with balsamic vinegar. Sprinkle the remaining oil over the soup. Garnish with basil leaves and serve at once.

Spaghetti with spinach and fried garlic

Serves 4

Ingredients

- 12½oz (400g) spaghetti
- 9½oz (300g) fresh spinach
- 8 cloves garlic
- 4tbsp (60ml) olive oil, cold pressed
- Salt as desired
- Freshly ground pepper as desired
- 1tbsp (15ml) butter
- Freshly grated parmesan (for garnish)

Method

1 Wash the spinach. Peel the garlic cloves and halve lengthways.

2 Cook the spaghetti in plenty of boiling, salted water until 'al dente'.

3 Heat 4tbsp (60ml) oil in a frying pan and gently fry the garlic until it is a golden yellow color. Take out of the pan and set aside. Put the wet spinach into the pan, cover with a lid and heat until the spinach is just done. Then steam over a high heat for about 1 minute. Season well with salt and pepper.

4 Drain the spaghetti and mix with the spinach, the garlic and the butter. Garnish with freshly grated parmesan.

Minestrone

Serves 4

Ingredients

- 11oz (350g) broad beans, frozen
- 3 beefsteak tomatoes
- 11oz (350g) carrots
- ½ celeriac bulb
- 2 sticks celery
- 2½oz (75g) spinach
- 3oz (150g) streaky bacon
- 2 onions
- 2tbsp (30ml) oil
- 4 potatoes
- 2½oz (80g) grated parmesan
- Salt & pepper as desired
- 2¼oz (70g) orecchiette (ear-shaped pasta)
- A few parsley leaves
- 1¾pints (1 litre) water
- Courgettes

Method

1 Scald the tomatoes, then refresh in cold water, skin, quarter, deseed and chop roughly. Thaw the beans. Peel, wash and dice the carrots and celeriac. Wash and drain the spinach. Trim, wash and slice the celery.

2 Dice the bacon and sauté in oil until transparent. Peel and finely chop the onions and sauté with the bacon until soft.

3 Peel, wash and finely dice the potatoes, add to the pan with the carrots, celeriac and celery and sauté for a few minutes, stirring. Add 1¾pints (1 litre) water and simmer for 20 minutes. Add the tomatoes, courgettes, beans, spinach and pasta, bring to a boil, cover with a lid and cook over a low heat for 15 minutes. Finely chop the parsley leaves, stir in and season the soup with salt and pepper. Serve sprinkled with parmesan.

Spinach gnocchi with ricotta and parmesan

Serves 4

Ingredients

- 8oz (250g) fresh spinach
- Salt as desired
- 8oz (250g) ricotta
- Grated nutmeg
- 1 egg
- 1 egg yolk
- 3½oz (100g) grated parmesan
- 5½oz (175g) flour and flour for the work surface
- 2-3tbsp (30-45ml) olive oil
- 3tbsp (45ml) butter

Method

1 Sort and wash the spinach and blanch in boiling, salted water for 2-3 minutes. Rinse the spinach in cold water, squeeze out well and chop very finely.

2 Whisk the ricotta, salt, nutmeg, egg, egg yolk, parmesan and spinach until smooth using the whisk attachment of an electric hand mixer. Stir in the flour using a wooden spoon. Add more flour, if necessary, to produce a light, malleable dough. Roll the dough (in portions) into strings ¾in (2cm) thick on a lightly floured work surface and divide the strings into ½-¾in (1-2cm) lengths. Press a pattern into the individual gnocchi with a fork if you wish.

3 Bring a large pan of salted water to the boil. Reduce the temperature and cook the gnocchi in the simmering water, a few at a time, for about 3 minutes. Take out with a slotted spoon or skimmer. Drain well, sprinkle with a little olive oil and cool.

4 Heat the butter in a frying pan, add the gnocchi and toss for 2-3 minutes. Serve garnished with grated parmesan and fresh spinach leaves.

Tomato and mozzarella crostini with olives

Serves 4

Ingredients

- 4 ripe tomatoes
- 8oz (250g) mozzarella
- 8 pitted olives
- 1 clove garlic
- 8 slices ciabatta
- A little dried oregano
- Salt & freshly ground pepper as desired
- Baking parchment

Method

1 Scald the tomatoes in boiling water for a few seconds, then refresh in cold water, skin and slice. Drain and slice the mozzarella. Halve the olives. Peel the garlic clove.

2 Rub the slices of bread with the garlic clove and sprinkle with a little oregano. Then top first with mozzarella, then with tomato slices and olives. Sprinkle with salt, pepper and oregano.

3 Line a baking tray with baking parchment. Lay the prepared crostini on the tray and put into a preheated oven [350ºF (180°C)] for about 10 minutes.

Chicken breast with spaghetti puttanesca

Serves 4

Ingredients

- 16oz (500g) tomatoes
- 2 cloves garlic
- 6 anchovy fillets in oil
- 1 small dried chilli
- 4tbsp (60ml) olive oil
- 3fl oz (100ml) dry red wine
- 4 chicken breast fillets
- 2tbsp (30ml) chopped herbs (thyme, rosemary, parsley)
- 12½oz (400g) spaghetti
- Salt & freshly ground pepper as desired
- 4tbsp (60ml) black olives

Method

1 Scald the tomatoes in boiling water for a few seconds, then refresh in cold water, skin, quarter, deseed and dice finely. Peel the garlic and chop finely with the anchovies and the chilli. Sauté the garlic mixture in oil. Add the tomatoes and wine and cook over a medium heat without a lid for about 15 minutes.

2 Season the chicken breast fillets with salt and pepper and fry on one side in an ovenproof grill pan until lightly browned. Turn, sprinkle with herbs and put into a preheated oven [350ºF (180°C)] for a further 10 minutes or so, until done.

3 Cook the spaghetti in plenty of boiling, salted water until 'al dente'. Mix the olives into the sauce and season to taste with salt and pepper. Drain the spaghetti, mix with the sauce and serve with the chicken breast fillets.

Ribbon pasta with almonds, courgettes and olives

Serves 4

Ingredients

- 6½oz (200g) mixed minced meat
- 1 clove garlic
- 4 chopped tomatoes
- 2tbsp (30ml) chopped almonds
- 10 black olives, without stones, cut into fine rings
- Salt as desired
- Freshly ground pepper as desired
- 2 yellow courgettes
- 3tbsp (45ml) olive oil
- 1 green courgette
- 9½oz (300g) fettuccine
- 8 black olives

Method

1 Heat the oven to 400°F (200°C).

2 Mix the minced meat with the tomatoes, almonds and olive rings. Season with salt and pepper.

3 Wash the yellow courgettes and halve lengthways. Scrape out the cores with a teaspoon. Fill the courgette halves with the mince mixture. Lay on a greased baking tray, sprinkle each with 1tbsp (15ml) olive oil and bake in the hot oven for about 20 minutes.

4 Thinly slice the green courgette lengthways with a potato peeler. Cook the pasta in plenty of salted water, until 'al dente' and drain. Mix the hot pasta with the green courgette ribbons and 2tbsp (30ml) olive oil. Add a little salt.

5 Arrange the pasta on plates with a stuffed courgette half on each plate and serve, garnished with black olives.

Fried potatoes with chanterelles

Serves 4

Ingredients

- 19oz (600g) cooked potatoes from the previous day (firm-cooking)
- 1 small carrot
- 2 small onions
- 1 clove garlic
- ½ bunch parsley
- 16oz (500g) chanterelles
- 3tbsp (45ml) clarified butter
- Salt & freshly ground pepper as desired
- A dash of dry white wine

Method

1 Peel and thickly slice the potatoes. Peel and finely dice the carrot. Peel the onions and garlic. Halve the onions and cut into strips. Wash the parsley and chop the leaves. Clean the chanterelles and cut the larger mushrooms in half lengthways.

2 Heat 2tbsp (30ml) clarified butter in a large frying pan and fry the potatoes and carrots over a medium heat, turning only occasionally, until the potatoes are nicely browned. Towards the end of the cooking time add the onions and fry until golden. Season with salt and pepper.

3 Heat the rest of the clarified butter in a second frying pan and fry the chanterelles for 3 minutes. Season with salt and pepper. Press the garlic directly into the pan. Deglaze the mushrooms with wine and continue frying until almost all the liquid has evaporated.

4 Mix the chanterelles and parsley with the potatoes. Fry for a minute, then season to taste and serve.

Ragout with orecchiette

Serves 4-6

Ingredients

- 6½oz (200g) onions
- 6 cloves garlic
- 1 tin peeled tomatoes [25oz (800g)]
- 11tbsp (165ml) olive oil
- 25oz (800g) boneless veal
- 5fl oz (150ml) white wine
- 8oz (250g) carrots
- 8oz (250g) courgettes
- 8oz (250g) aubergines
- 12½oz (400g) orecchiette (ear-shaped pasta)
- Salt & freshly ground pepper as desired
- 1 bunch of oregano
- Juice of 1 lemon

Method

1 Peel and finely dice the onions and garlic. Empty the tomatoes and their juice into a bowl and break up roughly with a fork.

2 Heat 3tbsp (45ml) olive oil in a wide pan and sauté the onions and garlic until translucent, then set aside.

3 In another pan heat 2tbsp (30ml) oil and sauté the meat on all sides until nicely browned (you will need to do this in 3 portions, adding more oil for each). Deglaze the last portion with the white wine. Add the meat with the wine and meat juices to the onions and garlic. Add the crushed tomatoes with their juice and season with salt and pepper. Bring to a boil and cook over a medium heat without a lid for 30—35 minutes.

4 Peel the carrots, trim the courgettes, cut both into quarters lengthways and then slice at an angle into ½in (1cm) slices. Trim and quarter the aubergines and slice at an angle into ¾in (2cm) slices.

5 Heat a frying pan over a high heat, add 5tbsp (75ml) olive oil and fry the aubergines on all sides for 4 minutes. Then add the courgettes and carrots and fry for a further 6 - 8 minutes. Set aside.

6 Cook the pasta in plenty of boiling, salted water until 'al dente', then drain and mix with 3tbsp (45ml) olive oil and a little pepper.

7 Pick the oregano leaves from their stalks and add to the veal ragout with the lemon juice and the vegetables. Reheat, check the seasoning and serve with the pasta.

Minestrone with pesto

Serves 4

Ingredients

For the minestrone

- 5oz (150g) cooked pasta shells ('al dente')
- 3 large carrots
- 1 yellow courgette or 1 green courgette
- 3tbsp (45ml) olive oil
- 1 onion
- 1 chilli (optional)
- 8oz (250g) white beans (canned)
- 8oz (250g) string beans (frozen or canned)
- 16fl oz (500ml) vegetable stock (home-made or instant)
- 1 large tin tomatoes
- Salt as desired
- Pepper as desired

For the pesto

- 1 peeled garlic clove
- 6½oz (200g) basil leaves
- 1¼oz (40g) pine nuts
- 8fl oz (¼ litre) olive oil
- 1tsp (5ml) salt
- 3½oz (100g) parmesan

Method

For the minestrone

1 Wash, peel and slice the carrots and set aside. Wash and slice the courgette and set aside.

2 Skin and finely chop the onion. Heat the oil in a large pan and sauté the onion over a medium heat until soft. If you prefer a spicy soup, add a chopped chilli to the diced onion.

3 Add the carrots, the drained white beans, the drained string beans and the hot vegetable stock. Add a tin of chopped tomatoes to the soup and season with salt and pepper. Finally add the courgette and the pasta shells and bring to a boil.

For the pesto

Put all ingredients apart from the parmesan into a liquidizer and puree. Then add the parmesan and puree briefly until the mixture resembles a paste.

Spaghetti with tomatoes and basil

Serves 4

Ingredients

- 12½oz (400g) spaghetti
- Salt as desired
- Freshly ground pepper as desired
- 22½oz (700g) tomatoes
- 2 cloves garlic
- 2 handfuls fresh basil leaves
- 2tbsp (30ml) olive oil, cold pressed
- Parmesan, freshly grated
- 2tsp (10ml) butter

Method

1 Wash the tomatoes, then scald, skin, halve, deseed and dice. Press the garlic cloves and mix with the diced tomatoes and 2tbsp (30ml) olive oil. Season with salt and pepper.

2 Cook the spaghetti in plenty of boiling, salted water until 'al dente' then drain, reserving 1 cupful of the cooking water. Mix the spaghetti with 2tsp (10ml) butter and 3-4tbsp (45-60ml) of the cooking water. Stir in the tomatoes and the basil leaves. Season with pepper and serve thickly sprinkled with parmesan.

Set mascarpone with brandy bread

Serves 4

Ingredients

- 10 sheets white gelatine
- 16oz (500g) mascarpone
- 3fl oz (100ml) milk
- 3fl oz (100ml) brandy
- 3tbsp (45ml) sugar
- 1tbsp (15ml) cocoa powder
- 3½oz (100g) sweet biscuits (e.g. petit beurre)
- 4 slices white bread (not too fresh)
- 1 egg
- Oil for frying
- 1-2tbsp (15-30ml) clear honey

Method

1 Soak the gelatine in cold water.

2 Push the mascarpone through a sieve and mix well with the milk, 1fl oz (30ml) brandy, sugar and cocoa.

3 Put the gelatine into a small pan dripping wet and dissolve over a low heat. Stir into the mascarpone cream, mixing well. Transfer the mixture to individual timbale moulds and put into the fridge for at least 3 hours.

4 Finely crush the biscuits with a rolling pin. Brush the slices of bread with the rest of the brandy. Whisk the egg and dip the slices of bread first in the egg and then in the crushed biscuits.

5 Heat the oil in a frying pan and fry the brandy bread on both sides until golden brown. Finally sprinkle with honey.

6 To serve, dip the timbale moulds briefly in hot water, turn the mascarpone out onto dessert plates and serve with the brandy bread.

Filled pastry shell

Serves 4

Ingredients

- ½ radicchio
- 1½oz (50g) preserving sugar
- ½ glass red wine
- 1½oz (50g) ricotta
- 1tbsp (15ml) Campari
- 12½oz (400g) cream
- 1½oz (50g) softened butter
- 1½oz (50g) icing sugar
- 1 egg white
- 1½oz (50g) flour
- 1tbsp (15ml) chopped pistachios
- Basil

Method

1 Wash and sort the radicchio and finely chop the leaves. Put into a pan with the preserving sugar and red wine and boil to a puree. Cool on a plate.

2 Add the ricotta and Campari to the puree. Whip the cream and fold in lightly. Cover and put in the refrigerator for 2 hours.

3 For the pastry shells, beat the softened butter with the icing sugar and the egg white.

4 Sieve the flour onto the mixture and slowly stir in. Line a baking tray with baking parchment. Spoon 2 thin circles [approximately 7in (18cm) in diameter] of the mixture onto the baking parchment. This will take about half of the mixture.

5 Bake in a preheated oven [400°F (200°C)] until the edges are beginning to brown (about 5 minutes). Take out of the oven immediately and carefully lay the wafers, while still soft, over upturned bowls or beakers, so that they will cool and harden in a bowl shape. Make 2 more pastry shells in the same way.

6 To serve, fill each pastry shell with radicchio puree, garnish with pistachios and basil leaves.

Mascarpone cream and fruit

Serves 4

Ingredients

- 3 figs
- 12½oz (400g) strawberries
- 2tbsp (30ml) sugar
- Juice of 1 orange
- 6fl oz (200ml) Vin Santo (Italian dessert wine)
- 1 vanilla pod
- 8oz (250g) mascarpone (Italian triple-cream cheese)
- 4oz (125g) quark (curd cheese, 20% fat)
- 2tsp (10ml) icing sugar (optional)
- 2½oz (75g) cantuccini (Italian almond biscuits)
- Mint for decoration

Method

1 Wash and quarter the figs. Wash and hull the strawberries and quarter if necessary. Put the sugar into a pan and let it melt without stirring. Stir in the orange juice and 3fl oz (100ml) Vin Santo and simmer for 5-6 minutes. Carefully stir in the strawberries. Remove the pan from the heat and chill the fruit.

2 Slit the vanilla pod open lengthways and scrape out the seeds. Mix with the mascarpone, the quark and the rest of the Vin Santo. Sweeten with icing sugar and chill. Crumble the biscuits.

3 Divide the mascarpone cream between 6 dessert plates. Add the fruit with a little of the sauce. Sprinkle with crumbled biscuits and decorate with mint.

Conversion guide

The Conversion guide given below is not an exact equivalent but an approximation, to make your measuring easier.

Dry Measures

Imperial	Metric
½oz	15g
1oz	30g
2oz	60g
3oz	90g
4oz (¼lb)	125g
5oz	155g
6oz	185g
7oz	220g
8oz (½lb)	250g
9oz	280g
10oz	315g
11oz	345g
12oz (¾lb)	375g
13oz	410g
14oz	440g
15oz	470g
16oz (1 lb)	500g
24oz (1½lb)	750g
32oz (2lb)	1Kg

Liquid Measures

Imperial	Metric
1fluid oz	30ml
2fluid oz	60ml
3fluid oz	100ml
4fluid oz	125ml
5fluid oz (¼pint /1gill)	150ml
6fluid oz	190ml
8fluid oz	250ml
10fluid oz (½pint)	300ml
16fluid oz	500ml
20fluid oz (1pint)	600ml
1¾pints	1000ml (1 litre)

Conversion guide

Cup & Spoon Measures

Imperial	Metric
¼tsp	1ml
½tsp	2½ml
1tsp	5ml
1tbsp	15ml
¼cup	60ml
½cup	125ml
1cup	250ml

Helpful Measures

Imperial	Metric
⅛in	3mm
¼in	6mm
½in	1cm
¾in	2cm
1in	2.5cm
2in	5cm
2½in	6cm
3in	8cm
4in	10cm
5in	13cm
6in	15cm
7in	18cm
8in	20cm
9in	23cm
10in	25cm
11in	28cm
12in	30cm

Oven temperatures

	°F (Fahrenheit)	°C (Celsius)	Gas Mark
Very low	250	120	1
Low	300	150	2
Moderately low	325	160	3
Moderate	350-375	180-190	4
Moderately hot	400-425	200-210	5
Hot	450-475	220-230	6
Very hot	500-525	240-250	7

Glossary

Al Dente In cooking, the adjective 'al dente' meaning 'to the bite' in Italian, describes pasta and rice that has been cooked so as to be firm but not hard. "Al dente" also describes vegetables that are cooked through but still offer resistance to the bite.

Anchovy is a a small fish usually stored in olive oil or salt. Anchovies are sold for flavoring.

Artichokes are European plants, cultivated for their large thistle-like flower-heads.

Basil also known as Sweet Basil has a strong, pungent, sweet smell. It is best when used fresh, and in cooked recipes, is generally added at the last moment, as cooking destroys the flavour quickly.

Basil pesto is a very versatile sauce made of basil, pine nuts, salt, olive oil, walnuts, garlic and curd or ricotta cheese. Pesto is commonly used in pasta & soups, on crackers and bread.

Beefsteak Tomatoes are the largest varieties of cultivated tomatoes, sometimes weighing 1 lb (½kg) or more. It is commonly used in sandwiches.

Balsamic Vinegar is an aromatic, aged vinegar traditionally manufactured in Modena, Italy, from the concentrated juice, or must, of white grapes. It is dark brown in color and its flavor is rich, sweet, and complex.

Cayenne Pepper The Cayenne is a hot red fruit used to flavor dishes; its name comes from the city of Cayenne in French Guiana. The fruits are generally dried, ground and sifted to make Cayenne pepper. Cayenne is used in cooking spicy hot dishes.

Campari is a pinkish aperitif flavored with bitters.

Capers are the cooked and picked flower buds of a bramblelike southern European shrub, used to flavor food.

Celery is a cultivated plant of the parsley family with closely packed succulent leafstalks that are eaten raw or cooked.

Celeriac also known as 'celery root,' 'turnip-rooted celery' or 'knob celery' may be used raw or cooked. It has a flavor similar to celery, so it is often used as a flavoring in soups and stews.

Chanterelle is an edible woodland mushroom with a yellow funnel-shaped cap and a faint smell of apricots, found in both Eurasia and North America.

Cherry tomato is a spherical miniature tomato. The fruit is glossy red, or occasionally yellow, and typically eaten in salad.

Ciabatta is a type of flattish, open-textured Italian bread with a floury crust, made with olive oil.

Cocktail tomatoes are slightly larger tomatoes which are rich red in colour. They are sold on the vine which makes them last much longer.

Courgettes or zucchinis, have a delicate flavor and can be appreciated with little more than a quick cooking with butter or olive oil, with or without fresh herbs. Zucchinis can be eaten raw, in a cold salad, as well as hot and barely cooked in hot salads.

Escalope Slices of boneless meat usually coated in egg and bread crumbs and then deep fried.

Fennel A culinary herb of the parsley family, it is grown for its dried, ripe fruits or seeds. They are widely used in Indian cuisine for their warm, sweet taste.

Fettuccine is a type of pasta. It is a very flat, thick noodle made of egg and flour, similar to tagliatelle.

Gorgonzola is a type of rich, strong-flavoured Italian cheese with bluish-green veins.

Mascarpone is a soft, mild Italian cream cheese.

Mozzarella is a mild, semisoft white Italian cheese, often used in Italian cooking as melted topping, especially on pizzas.

Nutmeg is the hard, aromatic, almost spherical seed of a tropical tree.

Parsley is used for its leaf in much the same way as coriander or cilantro, but has a milder flavor.

Pecorino is an Italian cheese made from ewes' milk.

Petit beurre is a creamy sauce made with butter, onions or shallots, as well as vinegar or lemon juice, usually served with seafood dishes.

Plum tomato is an Italian variety that is shaped like plum, typically used in cooking rather than raw.

Preserving sugar is a type of sugar that has very large crystals which dissolve quickly when stirred into a liquid, this reduces the risk of the sugar burning. Preserving sugar dissolves quicker than granulated sugar. Used in jams, jellies, marmalades and pickles where it dissolves quickly to give a good set.

Quark (Curd cheese) is a fresh cheese made from pasteurized milk. It is soft, white and unaged, similar to cream cheese.

Radicchio is a variety of chickory, that has dark red leaves.

Recchiette is a type of pasta native to Apulia, whose shape resembles a small ear.

Ricotta is an Italian whey cheese, meaning a product made from whey—a by-product of milk cheese making—rather than whole milk.

Rocket A deliciously peppery salad plant.

Romaine Lettuce is a variety of lettuce which grows a long head of sturdy leaves with a firm rib down the center. Unlike most lettuces, it is tolerant of heat.

Saffron is a spice derived from the flower of the saffron crocus. It is sold dried and used in cooking as a seasoning and coloring agent.

Shallots are commonly used in Thailand and come in all sizes and colors, including purple. If shallots aren't available at your local grocery store, or are too expensive, a good substitute would be a combination of white cooking onion and garlic.

Streaky bacon comes from the belly of a pig. It is very fatty with long veins of fat running parallel to the rind. This is the most common form of bacon in the United States.

Vin Santo is an Italian dessert wine. This traditional Tuscan wine is made from Trebbiano and Malvasia grapes, and is typically very sweet.

White gelatin is a virtually colorless tasteless water-soluable protein prepared from collagen and used in food preparation as the basis of jellies.

White wine vinegar is a pale, slightly pungent vinegar made from white wine. It is the base for many herb vinegars.